Entire Dilemma

Also by Michael Burkard

In a White Light 1977

None, River 1979

Some Time in the Winter (chapbook) 1979

Ruby for Grief 1981

The Fires They Kept 1986

Fictions from the Self 1988

My Secret Boat 1990

*My Brother Makes a Toast but Uses
by Mistake His Name* (chapbook) 1992

Three (chapbook) 1997

Entire Dilemma POEMS Michael Burkard

Sarabande Books Louisville, Kentucky

Managing Editor
Sarabande Books, Inc.
2234 Dundee Road, Suite 200
Louisville, KY 40205

Cover painting: *Untitled* by Mary
Hackett, from the collection of Keith
Althaus and Susan Baker. Used with kind
permission of the owners.

Cover and text design by
Charles Casey Martin.

Manufactured in the United States
of America.

This book is printed on acid-free paper.

Sarabande Books is a nonprofit
literary organization.

LIBRARY OF CONGRESS
CATALOGING-IN-PUBLICATION DATA

Burkard, Michael, 1947–
Entire dilemma : poems /
by Michael Burkard. — 1st ed.
        p.   cm.
ISBN 1-889330-17-5 (alk. paper). —
ISBN 1-889330-18-3 (pbk. : alk. paper)
I. Title. PS3552.U718E58 1998
811'.54—dc21   97-47221
                CIP
ISBN 978-1-889330-18-1

for Nancy Mitchell

Acknowledgments

Grateful acknowledgment is made to the following publications in which some of these poems first appeared: *ackee*, "Love's Money"; *The American Poetry Review*, "Entire Dilemma," "Stalin," "The Tenderness," "Goodbye," and "Ghost-Harm"; *The American Voice*, "The Boy Who Had No Shadow"; *Calliope*, "Driving Through Her Father with the Desert"; *Caprice*, "How to Ask" and "When Sal Died"; *Epoch*, "The Spellers" and "The Summer"; *Exquisite Corpse*, "Mel"; *Faultline*, "Where People Took Mary"; *The Gettysburg Review*, "Another Infinity"; *The North American Review*, "You: My Friend, My"; *Number One*, "A Point"; *Panoply*, "Sober Ghost" (under the title "Katya"); *The Paris Review*, "Before the Dark" and "But Beautiful"; *The Plum Review*, "Your Sister Life"; *Provincetown Arts*, "For Mary Hackett"; *Shankpainter*, "The Summer after Last"; *Volt*, "How I Shaded the Book"; *Zone 3*, "Picture of the Blueberry Money," "If You Please," "The Job," "The Man Who Made the Wallet," and "Star Held in Eye."

Grace Paley excerpt from *Enormous Changes at the Last Minute*, © 1960 Farrar, Straus, Giroux.

"But Beautiful," "How I Shaded the Book," "The Summer after Last," and "Your Sister Life," appear in the anthology *Last Call: Poems on Alcoholism, Addiction, and Deliverance*, edited by Sarah Gorham and Jeffrey Skinner, Sarabande Books, 1997.

"The Boy Who Had No Shadow" was reprinted in *ackee*.

"Entire Dilemma" appears in the anthology *Library Bound: A Saratoga Anthology*, edited by Linda Bullard, Saratoga Springs Public Library, 1996.

I would like to express my thanks to Michael Gervasio, Sarah Gorham, Mary Alice Johnston, Chris Kennedy, Ed Ruchalski, Malena Mörling, JoEllen Kwiatek, Shreerekha Pillai, Jeffrey Skinner, Michael Paul Thomas, and Diane Wald. Thanks also to Jay Boissy, Jennifer Colville, Eugene Newman, and Ada Richardson for sources for poems. And some light in return to Jeffrey Casazza and Kristen Casazza.

Contents

"I would like you to write a simple story just once more," he says, "the kind de Maupassant wrote, or Chekhov, the kind you used to write. Just recognizable people and then write down what happened to them next."

I say, "Yes, why not? That's possible." I want to please him, though I don't remember writing that way. I *would* like to try to tell such a story, if he means the kind that begins: "There was a woman..." followed by plot, the absolute line between two points which I've always despised. Not for literary reasons, but because it takes all hope away. Everyone, real or invented, deserves the open destiny of life.

—Grace Paley,
A Conversation with My Father

Fred,
I don't know what to do.
About me and you and the dream
which knocks and knocks at me, now has
me consistently in dream's time:
am completely in belief then
hapless

realize,
of course,
dream, dream,
it's only a dream. So: here you are,
with me, not quite, after a quarter of a century,
and I am simply missing you
as I have been prone to do, especially

since being sober.
For you were one of the few lives I have felt
I walked away from, never wanting to,
although realizing that it might have
happened regardless, and, also,
you may have had a part
in parting too.

Have you ever dreamed me?

*

Before the dark
I moved the glass
from the edge of the bureau

so that in the dark
I will not walk and reaching for an edge
knock the glass.

And when I close her door
which is also mine
I always have to take her bag
from the door
—otherwise the door
just might not close
and I would have to do it over again.

This too is before the dark.

*

Dreams, Fred, may not be a sign to get in touch.
They may be just the opposite.

When I write a letter home it's painful to be personal
because it never seems read that way, or answered.

I don't do it all the time. I've gotten used to that.
One gets more used to the moon when one knows one is a piece of it.

One more road for belief, or trust,
even if there isn't an answer.

14

Dreams may be just the opposite:
gateways through which a you or me could pass

without having answered ourselves.
As if we are signposts, take one step more.

Perhaps my brother has seen a dream like this,
or approximated whom he has dreamed most in time,

and thus whom he is closest to
in being.

I do not know if my brother has such thoughts,
and less often take the attitude he ought to.

But you, Fred,
did you ever say *before the dark,*

and mean anything other than evening?
Yes, most likely.

I have not heard your voice for a quarter of a century
but I can hear you say it, *before the dark,*

and mean evening, or night just before the final light
goes off, and still something slightly more.

*

Rain on a trailer-roof.
Train passing nearby on track beside lake.

Fred and Sue, Marco…
and the evening for me which would be
my parting from them.
Except for a year later, again in rain,
Fred visiting town, stopping me on the street
from his car, and in that tone of his which
was real and true: "You're not really getting
married, are you?" He, like me, knew it was
too soon, so soon, that there was some
unnamed-by-everyone trouble for me.
I knew too.

*

Last words:
time and time again.

Neighbors entering
the yard at dusk,

hanging around,
dark coming.

Their voices
got quieter in the dark.

Their shirts were not sparks
but little dots seemed

to begin to move
around. Quiet.

Last words.
Time and time

again spring
entered winter.

I wanted to stay put,
oh for just once,

where I was.
But went off.

Leave the town
slowly or it will

tear you up,
maybe even to pieces.

People like Fred had
something I wanted,

if I knew what to call it
I would. Last words.

I wanted to stay put,
smell the spring,

just that. Not move,
let someone know me.

Make neighbors
of spring—make

before the dark
a ring of friendship.

Maybe that's why
the neighbors literally

milled around,
a little like animals

at a water hole,
a little awkward,

a little wondering
where to go next

and just when.
Sparks! It is possible

that in gazing at the moon
a time or two they became

the moon for just a moment.
Light translated between

the few of them and the moon.
And me a part of being

also. Whether there
or apart, before the dark

or not. Last words:
dream on, dream on,

whatever it may mean.
There's a name there

unnamed by everyone.
Fred

is one
of many names.

✖ THE TENDERNESS

A few dark dealers of cards
stand in one's face.
A card is missing
(the tenderness you dream you hate).

Teachers are mean.
Their tenderness falls asleep .
halfway through the class.
You took out a deck of cards

in order to survive.
You were punished.
Sent home.
Abolished.

In those days
one did not have to do much
in order to be abolished.
And now this:

a few dark dealers of cards
breathe in one's face.
A card is missing
(the tenderness you dream you hate).

✖ HOW I SHADED THE BOOK

I was in the town before my end. I knew more deeply
than before I was in trouble with drinking.
I received a copy of a Graham Greene novel, *The End of the Affair*, in the mail.
I sat down to read it one night, sure I would not like it,
but I could not stop reading.
I felt the romance of the book was validating one more wild prolonged fling,
alcohol at the center of the fling. I had no one in mind but I knew there
     would be
someone. And I knew it would be trouble.
The novel made me feel as if I could see it all.

In the middle of the night there was a knock on the door.
A neighbor—I had met no one in the few days I had been in town—
asked if I would drive her and her daughter to the hospital.
Her daughter was sick, she had no car. She had seen my light.
For some reason I was glad to do so. I took the book.
The wait was long, the mother finally told me I could leave,
she could call a relative if they had to leave the hospital.

I saw them on the street days later—she hardly spoke—I wondered if it
     was because
we were of different races. She simply nodded when I asked if her daughter
was all right.
They left their house within a month. The house became a place for
     itinerants.
Six families in six months. One afternoon I heard screaming and cackling
and looked out the window to see an overweight man who could hardly walk

21

limping and tilting away from the old woman on the porch.
She both screamed and cackled. The overweight man finally
hobbled off like an old wagon.

I want to thank the woman and her child for interrupting my reverie.
Although I proceeded to wildly continue an affair for drinking
I feel that couple as a pull from life, a pull
from a source I was for a final time denying.
The book meant more than life. How I shaded the book
meant more than anything, anyone.

⚹ NEXT TO THE LAMP OF A PANTHER

Books in the cellar
next to a lamp of a panther.
After hours he stands there

beside himself
wishing he were an elf
who could not read

or write: life,
he writes,
would have been much simpler.

It simply isn't true.
Married people do not have
to go to school

but he did not marry.
He played the fool,
wrote, collected books,

antiques and lamps,
went off to school
again long after school

was through, and generally
had a common life.
One is not so unique.

One is never quite
original enough, or
finished. Even this

wish, recurrent, to be
elf-life or to possess
a slightly other than human

magic isn't so far-
fetched. It's a
sensible or harmless

compensation given
one's powerlessness.
Like keeping the books

in the cellar, next to
a lamp of a panther,
to keep them in their

place.

✖ THE ANNIVERSARY

after Paul Klee's "Red-Brown and Violet-Yellow Rhythm"

I don't know exactly what Klee meant,
I'm not even sure if he meant anything "exactly."
I found a definition of "no."
Like childhood? Like a star in the night too.

If I stayed a worker at the hospital all these years
I would now have the choice of getting out early
(red-brown) with a pension intact. I know this sounds
a little ridiculous (violet-yellow), but I am saying

all this tomorrow, not today, because I am convinced
(orange-black) (and tomorrow came upon us unexpectedly,
like Klee) because I am convinced
tomorrow is the day we would now meet for the first time
in our lives. I know I stayed at the hospital less

than three years (blue-blue), and I know it is now
twenty-seven or so years later. I know I've known you
since 1975. But if I had just stayed, we would now just
be meeting. And without other writers around, and without
crazy trains we're thinking we're supposed to take or

take as images (yellow-white) for our separate lives.
So: I have money in my pocket (retirement party, brown-red),
and money in my mind (pension and other illusions), and
I am in a mood to spend. Poetry is very far from my mind

(black-pink), maybe because I am no longer the hospital
worker who also doubles as closet poet by co-workers. Non-
descript. And: I am turning a corner in the city when I
hear your voice (blue-brown): "I can't make out his face

when he is like this."
And I see you with the telephone. And I have the year
wrong (black-white), and I have the starry night wrong.
And it never was a childhood anyway, nor was Klee
childhood. But I know who you are now, across

all the times you have been told to change your voice.
Across all the times your brother has flown across
Peru. Across all the times I have had nothing (white-
white) to say, but I must, I insist, say it to you.

—for Diane

✖ WHEN SAL DIED

When Sal died
his son read a passage about a bird
which could still fly,
even when the branch broke.

When Lester died
I wanted to sing at his wake.
He would have liked that,
so would have I.

When loves die
you do think of birds,
you think of many trees,
many years.

You think of singing,
and sighing,
and many songs
over the years.

What the songs meant,
what the birds meant.
When light hit the window
and someone was near

yet far,
for this was life.

When Nellie was courted
in Nova Scotia,

when Teresa was courted
in Sicily.
Foggy Nova Scotia,
sunny Sicily.

When the son and the daughter
went out into the world.
When the piano sighed
just a little bit.

I think I will be quiet
now. I would like
to read that passage
about the bird.

—for Salvador Frumento, 1918–1989

✳ A POINT

All you need is a point.
It seems that it has no dimension.
But that point can become God.
Any God.

—And so the man stopped.
The road glistened in the rain.
Sex was shining for someone
somewhere on the block.

And the woman sat there, at the back
of her store, wondering why
she never bought the house,
the small white one across the river.

And the other man thought about
the limits of confession,
brother against brother,
river to river—

one could end up at a point
and still not
be at the end
—end is such a small drop

like the end in sex,
the end of buying,
the end of the house
where the brothers lived.

✖ GHOST-HARM

No one saw me then, or much of me. I was like a figure in hiding from the cover of a children's book: always among trees, among fences, bushes, backs of buildings close to the sea. It was usually night because it would be night before I would go there.

"There" was your place, although your place always stayed across the high street, and always two flights up. Only one time was it another place: accidentally one afternoon as I heard a commotion outside of the small half of a house I was house-sitting in, outside the small bedroom window, I looked and saw a commotion of people, and an ambulance which had not raised its siren on its way, and a man standing who looked like he knew what he was doing, who looked in some vague way like my brother, or a brother of mine, a could-have-been-a-brother-of-mine if not like my literal brother.

The coincidence is it was him who you were then with, unknown to me though, although something in me could have known I guess.

When one is as self-centered as a planet one can lurk in the dark like I did, pretty harmless to others because of a willingness to keep a distance, literal and otherwise, but who knows if some minor ghost-harm is being inflicted on one's own or not.

I am thinking of planets in orbit. Lives orbiting other lives. Insatiable. Intangible. Brothers to love from a distance or close up.

This isn't art. This is life.

✖ PROSE NOIR

my prose is claustrophobic
my prose is mathematical
my prose is my mother's hand
my prose buys a face
my prose is lost life
my prose is Raddy
my prose is the eggman who hands me pennies
    from the real world of Tom's five-year-old
my prose is the uncle moon and Alberti's visitor
    from still another moon
my prose is noir
    goggles
    unsung sex

�֍ STALIN

The mother and daughter
appeared in the dream
as two harbors. Both
were aflame, at a door.
The son and brother
who dreamed them told them
to step back, they must
be mistaken. And then
within the dream he recalled
wondering how fire could ever
be mistaken.

But he had time to only
wonder for a moment.
For a storm had disguised
itself as a giant bird.
This giant bird ate children,
and could reach as high
as the sun and the moon.
The giant bird pecked at both.
And then sad cabbages
floated in the harbor,
on their way to sea.

Power is bankrupt, but has
devastating consequences.

Like glass one has to wear
as a stocking.

To break us.
To create gloom.
To make death reasonable.

To have a voice which will
utter a new direction.

Have you eaten yet today,
my people?

Yes. We have been nourished
by your sad cabbages of death.

*

Perhaps the woman from our youth,
the stranger who appeared now and then
to help, told us she had a "cabbage head"
not to explain her scars on her neck,
but to quietly and ever so indirectly
inform us something of what was and what
would come.

This stranger was helpful, and now
it does seem like a useful piece of information.

✖ TOM

Thomas.
No light.
A street.
A house.
A family which
offered meals
to any one.
Thomas.
Name of one
friend. Name
of oven too
which singed
first love's
mother's hair.
First love?
Maybe not.
One clocks
somewhere in
and out of
time. To
honor
Thomas,
to honor
Tom. Mary's
son, one
living, one
dead.

✗ WHERE PEOPLE TOOK MARY

Is Tom living in Mary's house
all by himself? Is the upstairs
just as dark? Is the tallest tree
on Nickerson Street still there
where the small yard begins
and ends, where people took Mary
all kinds of dark, stories she
wanted most of all to tell.

✗ THE BOY WHO HAD NO SHADOW

One thing led to another:
if I have no shadow
I will eventually be followed
by those who do have shadows.
Sooner or later they will greet me
at the river and, judging me
as peculiar, will shove me into the river
to drown.

And the boy who had no shadow was correct.
But before he was shoved into the river,
days and days before, he was asked innocent
questions by innocent bystanders:
"Does your mother have a shadow?"
"Were you conceived in shadow?"
"Are you perhaps your own version
of your own shadow?"

And them were difficult questions
because he had no answer
—or, the boy who had no shadow
had no answer.

So they thought he was up to no good.
The questions became less innocent.

And because, by now, he was also judged
as not belonging to any crucial historical epoch,
he was shoved into the river
and kept beneath the surface by poles.

Not a particularly unique circumstance.
But the reason was unique and they knew that.
So, just to be sure, just to be sure
the boy had no shadow, they kept him down for days.

Lest the shadow which he had not,
which he had been murdered for,
escape in the river and flee.

✖ HOW TO ASK

Seeing the black/yellow
coverleaf of the Kafka
book I gave away,
now forgotten, until

sitting in their house,
in a certain chair,
looking up in a certain
way to realize I want

this book, among many
I "gave away," I
want this book back,
how to ask, how to

sit listening to conversation
among the three of us
when most of all I want
this Kafka back.

Things which have no boundary.
The momentum of very old ways.

Things: a collective word which is hated by some perfectionists.
One of those words which just sort of loosely points,
says over here,
maybe.

Maybe not.
What is wrong with the word.

It occurs to everyone.
Perhaps that is what is wrong with "things."

Things has no boundary.
Oh, we assume so, but no,
it doesn't.

And:
it doesn't wear a hat.
It doesn't sing.
It probably doesn't desire algebra.

It may be related to algebra,
which would explain its impatience.

Because it is impatience.
Have you ever seen things in the twilight?
Not as calm as you think.

Anxious to get somewhere, anywhere.
Been waiting all day for twilight.

And because it doesn't have a song
things is moving on.
Out there.

Following the sun and the moon
into space.

⚔ THE JOB

What was it worth,
and why were you doing it?
Was it the money,
was it the wife?

Was it a year from yesterday
when you heard those words
from memory which told you
never to look a gift horse

in the mouth? Except
this wasn't a horse,
this was the job,
there wasn't any horse

to look in the mouth
because you were too busy
feeding yourself. And there
certainly wasn't anything

left over for a gift.
Species after species
is dying. And here you
sit, on the job. Sometimes

you stand on the job, even
when you can't stand it.
What was it worth,
and why were you doing it?

THE MAN WHO MADE THE WALLET

He took three days, or so memory tells him.
It was stitched, and awkwardly red.
But perhaps the awkwardness was overcome by the primitive feeling
it had in the hands, the hands felt more primitive for holding it.
And the man liked that.

The man gave it to another,
just as he had intended.
And it was contentedly received, accepted,
the acceptance did not seem passive,
or so memory tells him. Although now the moment is a little suspect.

But not then.
The world was wide when the man accepted the wallet
from the other man. The trees were never so beautifully passive
for both of them: green trees were green from the winter window,
somehow still as in a dream. And blue trees were never
more blue in their silence.

When the man returned the wallet a few days later
he did so by saying perhaps the man who made the wallet would
like to have it.
The man who made the wallet made no protest, asked no questions.

Memory tells him this is all there is to say,
there is no moment of the wallet after this.

There were moments after moments for both the men
but none ever seemed quite the same.

Awkwardly red—that is what the man remembers most.
And he wonders what the other man remembers.

✖ PRAYER

My dog
who disappeared,
may you sleep soundly
in the form of this
cat I found, have
taken in to heal,
address as being in
league with you and
your form, until all
or much is mended.

Mr. Nobody stood in his doorway—
no one there in that night.

Another night, who knows?—someone
like your old sister might be stopping
in the dark to knock and knock,

until you tell her
"no."

"No"—a sound like the wind
if you want it to be...

just say so,
try it.

If you're thinking of her now
it's raining, and she's asleep,
in some little town

you haven't found yet.
No. You found the place years ago,

you were there.
They said so, you agreed.

You left
to see

if you could know her from afar.
And a town, a star.
A sentimental reason

to say "no one."
Your sister life will find a way
of supporting just about any

of your own conclusions.
Stopping in the dark
to knock and knock.

She's there.
You don't have to let her in.

✕ MEL

Who the hell is Mel?
He's the guy sitting next to your government
representative so your representative won't
say the wrong thing to you about the union.
So no wonder Mel only mumbles his
last name, and when you wake up laughing but
sweating in the night you say Who the hell
is Mel? with a kind of sincerity you couldn't
have dreamt of, and he is in your hometown
to boot, shit, there are Mels and have been
Mels in hometowns like yours
since this whole usury and demos thing
got started. Take a memo: a series of
murders entitled THE MEL MURDERS. Can't
you hear the readers-to-be in the shop now:
Who the hell is Mel? Cut. Print.
Take.

✘ MY SOCKS

Are not your socks.
They are my socks,
whether you or I
or anyone else out
there with a claw
or calling or not
likes it. Have

enjoyed my socks
more than I can
say—not unlike
my neighbor's joy
which is unknown
to me or you or
even my in-laws—
but somewhere in

the steamy after-
noon or night my
neighbor's having
a joy or two, or
if plural then more
than simple pleasures
—by any measure
of my life or yours
my neighbor's joys

have more than likely
or distantly

totaled in the thou-
sands. Maybe close
to the times I have
worn my socks.

✖ UNSEEN FALLING

Forty-seven years ago,
in 1943, the young boy
fell in love with a pencil.
It was a few weeks

after his father died,
suddenly, away, not at
war, but at a hotel,
at war with himself.

The young boy's pencil
—not aware of the love—
enlisted. It fell off
a desk in basic training,

an unseen falling, and
never saw war, but was
also never returned.
The young boy is an old man

by some standards
before he tells this story.
A secret kept for fifty
years or more.

Not much of a secret now.
Not much of a boy.

Except he's telling everyone.
His listeners knoweth not

where truth begins or ends
or when the ledge falls off.
Some remain ignorant,
meaning they tell others

about the man now.
Others, fewer, wonder
about the pencil. An ex-
wife, an old friend,

one of them feels
peculiarly betrayed.
And still one more,
one exhausted night,

puts binoculars to the stars,
and is thrown by the more
rapid fluctuating of light.
Millions of years old.

No two pencils are exactly
alike. Like identities.
Like years and wars with
self or others. Like wives

and friends and x-s.
Like seven other brothers

and sisters, all of whom
received the news also,

but, as far as we know,
did not find it necessary
to fall in love
with a pencil.

And pencil, wherever you
are, if you are,
may it cheer you
to know your secret

is out. It was never
that startling a secret,
but time has a way,
time has a way.

✖ THE SUMMER AFTER LAST

I do not want to belabor invisibility,
but if it isn't there in the spaces
among the people as a spiritual thread
then I do not want to be there either.

Sea or no sea, house or not.

There is a useless rage in returning
to the past. It is a labor
not unlike labor among the stones,
5 years time and someone is made to break them
for nothing.

Sea or no sea, house or not.

In the unrational time of the summer
after last I found myself alone
with the sun, simple night,
water when I wanted water.
My heart almost broke for not
being used to this.

It is amazing, the chains attempted
upon the heart.

Sea or no sea, house or not.

—for Bill

✖ PICTURE OF THE BLUEBERRY MONEY

Her life is no longer earnest.
It is like the blueberry money,
lost, or for the time being
misplaced on a shelf, hidden

in a boring drawer beneath
a boring story, or left so
obviously in the open no eye
will see it, because the eye

is clutching such a desperate
picture of the blueberry money
it can only picture a forest,
a stranger's arm around her back,

a glade with a stream beside it
and Fanny's grandson Jim smiling,
Fanny whom she knew years and
years ago, Jim whom she has never

known, and she realizes she will
live here forever, underground,
with the stranger who only has
to teach eight hours a week and

so has plenty of time to work
on love, with her, and they can

too seek the blueberry money
in an underworld, truly there has

never been an underworld so like
this, of green.

✗ LOVE'S MONEY

Colder than cold.
Coldest
when you board the bus,
among other wet bus-people,
and have to reach for it.

Not cold enough.
Not fulfilling enough.

And it doesn't please God,
love's money.
Because it has the face
of a beaten horse.
Or the horse has become
a good actor
and remains silent.

Your mother is a good actor,
and it is no coincidence that she is riding with you.

And now you know that when
you asked for your friend's address,
he was not your friend.
What you wanted was his toy, his telephone,
and his money.

And he knows that now too.
Just as surely as he sat there
on that bus with his mother
when you asked him for love's money.

✗ THE SPELLERS

Two friends,
spellers.

One lies, just enough, about how many books he's read,
and the town gives him many ribbons.
The other's total number of books read
is close,
but not close enough.

Before they read they had to be spellers,
today, the day of the ribbons,
it is enough that they are just readers.

Two readers,
friends.

And a third reader, just up ahead of them,
in another category, who reads even more...

and she enjoys even more
for she has received more books
instead of ribbons.

And on the third day she rose again from the dead
and laughed and named all the books she was given.

Let's face it:
the dead are given many books.

If there were to be a fire in the alphabet tonight
one would not want to be a *z*, an *m*, a *c* . . .
who knows where it would begin . . .

and one would not want to be a speller
—maybe not even a friend.

For friends lie. A friend can spell himself
out of a tight corner.

And then the fire comes, and then the shadow,
and who knows which is which.

✸ ENDINGS

Her second justifiably angry husband
is mulling the woods again. She is mulling
the *mull* in mulling when she sees him there.
His vocabulary is static, he is not as handsome as he was,
he may have had an affair once or twice or more.
He's a drag.

She's living miles away in Idaho.
The job is sweet, the people like her.
And once in a while she wants to enter the woods
to dine with strangers and see if the torches
she divines can indeed be found.

✕ IF YOU PLEASE

People on streets:
o lay me down
to no disease,
and if you please

break her heart.
For she left me
for a trolley
an hour ago or

more, and it rains
now and then,
and now and then
it pours.

The summer was full of boxes,
even though the family wasn't moving.

It was the summer umbrellas refused to open,
hands refused to close.

The youngest boarder cheated at cards,
even though no money was at stake.
He denied cheating.
It was tiresome.

The uncle was suffering from diabetes.
It was acting up,
he did not take good care of himself.
Three times a week he headed into the town
on Pern Hamp's truck.

Well, it wasn't a truck and it wasn't a bus.
It was more like the cab of a truck
with a box in back of it.

There were few cars,
no buses, so almost everyone
rode with Pern Hamp.

Even children rode.
And even by themselves.

And when they climbed into the semidark
of the box they did not know just what
they saw or what they were thinking,
but they thought "This smells like war."

And because it did smell like war
war was no longer funny.

The box contained men who suffered
from diabetes and were poor,
and dirty men, and many men.
And the men seemed mean in the semidark.
And it made sense for a child to think
maybe he should be mean too.

And each person was separated from another
by no more than a foot.

✗ YOU: MY FRIEND, MY

It is nice to know
letters arrive when
you least expect
them: this one

indicts our president
and rightly so.
Someone has to
indict him and it

might as well be
you: my friend, my
lover of blues, my
least-expected-letter-

writer who has a
thing or two to say
and says it, and I'm
here. I like it.

I like the stamp
too—the gentle
deer, the moon
behind the single

deer with a black
stick in front of

the moon like a
flag of a country

a century after
peace.

—for H.

How dark, but you never kneeled there.
Lightbulbs, plural, shining through drawn
curtain on hot day, early spring, time
changing. Two boys in the next house making
noise, noise of April, every April since . . .
Whenever that space darkens in the middle
of the day, that house-space, no birds
flying there, you want to tell stories
which would make people kneel. You are
not even sure what that means. You are
sure of one story. A man you had met who
had years before turned over in the hot
desert on his stomach and then his back
and pleaded to no one but the heart for
help, the heat. And to leave much too
much out years later when he tells you
he spelled Krazy Kat with a 'K' instead
of the correct 'C' and was humiliated
by the teacher for this

—no, that is not the story.
He is asked among the others in the class
if anyone can spell "cat." He begins to
spell it with a K and is laughed at. But
the teacher is sure he is joking. So she
asks him again, and again he spells it
Kat. He knows he is correct because of

68

the comics' Katzenjammer Kids. It makes
sense. But now he is upset and the laugh
is really at him, and the teacher makes
him stand there again and again, spelling
it, without relief, till the space darkens
with a scream. It would be easy to dream
some night of a Kul-de-sac like this one,
to get it wrong, based on someone else's
life, to have them there screaming or
laughing—the boys and the lightbulbs—
but to have him beside you as a companion
in your mistake, as founder of your mistake

—no, that is not the story.
But this is the way it ends.

✗ ANOTHER INFINITY

The railroad cars are infinite in the stolen light of the moon.
The relationship has ended: the world has shoved off into another infinity,
where there is not a name for anything.

One moment more for either my father's sperm or my mother's egg and
        the gates may
have closed. A few more moments and I might not ever even be thought of,
or someone like me with just a part of my face and a part of my leg might
        be walking
up a hill in Peru, hearing another kind of stone, walking to the roadside
        grave of
a feather and a bird
which would be me
in the life
if the gates had closed.

In an overdone painting of Jesus talking with children in the hills
there is a pilgrim standing down a hill, and Jesus and the children have
        their backs
turned, and the pilgrim stands there with a black mark for a face
staring, staring from a stone fence. One child
has his entire head turned in the direction of the pilgrim,
I'm given this wonderful insight into his hair
and I wonder if his face is blank.

So blank a railroad car could uncouple and inhabit it,
so blank a black mark for a face could exchange its place.

And I wonder about "I," who has nothing to do with this.
And my mother and father in the railroad dark.
I am linked irrevocably with everyone and everything,
and yet I do not exist.

And what is even more reassuring
is that I miss you, immensely, just as the stolen light
will miss me
until another time.

The money's too low and the time too short.
The woman didn't stutter her entire life for this.
The evergreens wear hooded vests in the forests of the snow
and that's more for her than a job. It's more

than the cages domestic birds arrive in, more
than the time she had no home.
What a life: she is driving through her father with the desert
and a soul who's inhabited the desert enters her.

Not painful,
not fearful.
Odd like a light
when you don't need one.

✖ STAR HELD IN EYE

God so loved the world
He gave his only begotten
pail of milk, and a mule
to transport it.

Witness the world late
at night: Mary may be dead
or not. Someone may know,
but far away we do not.

A little travel,
a star held in eye
like gossip held in brains.
A circumstance

guaranteeing a kind
of identity, accurate
or not, beholden to
no one.

Least of all the world.
Or God. Or the mule
who has transported it
for too long a time.

✕ MY CONSTRUCTOR

Maybe ten, maybe twenty
envelopes. Securing them with bands.
Led to sleep.
Led to vision of being with
contemporary-yet-ancestral "friend."
Who knew what to do, how to do:

stretching animals—
chickens, hens, foxes, cows, dogs—
to their maximum alive
(and they had to remain alive,
we were not to kill them
in the stretching of them)

—constructing them in the shape/feel
of a barn door,
as one like us
might construct a series of tightly
knit
doors with string.

And the whole point was to stretch
the animals but keep them alive,
for otherwise another tribe could
set them afire, invade us.
Alive, though stretched in pain,
the animals had a power

—would protect our tribe.
And toward the end I got
the hang of it, although
I gulped when latching a fox's
foot tightly as I could.
Foot stretched so far its skin

broke. We were carpenters?
Phil, Dennis, Dennis-son: these
are plays on the name of my
companion. My constructor.
Vision ended quietly enough,
a simple sense of "now done."

Night was like a gigantic fire.
Not that night was on fire or
full of flames. Just that night
was vast, that fire was vast,
that it was a long time ago.
That we were fearful, but pleased.

✖ BUT I BUY THE SHIRT

The man says to me
"It's van Gogh's shirt."
I know it isn't, but
this man has no earthly
reason to say this, least
of all to me—a blonde
fan of painter's letters,
an ebony fan of shirts,
a blue devotee of
interviews with the living.
But I buy the shirt,
for too much agony has
enveloped all of us—
me, the man, the woman,
van Gogh (we know),
agony, cheap rhymes,
forsaken shirts.

✖ A KISS AND A STAR

When I am vulnerable
I am again standing
in the cafeteria, next
to Grace, attempting
to be comfortable
among strangers of
a different ilk: but

I slip and kiss her
face without the proper
invitation. And the
silence is so loud
inside my head that
even across the years
I wonder what was

I doing, or trying
to do—was this kiss
a blessing or a curse—
or a blank—a blank
star?—a star which
breathes, at last?—
at last?

✗ SOBER GHOST

My mother, Nettie, and her sister, Lelia,
heard, as children, the ghost of their Aunt Anna's feet
shuffling across the upstairs floors.
Upon a timid and frightened inspection
they would, of course, find no one.
Lelia insists they heard Anna's bedroom window close
—my mother never agreed.

I never walked with either mother or Aunt Lelia under the stars at night.
Anna I pretended walked with me, through the grass, across the white river
which flows a few hundred yards behind the apple trees.
This was my version of walking with the dead. I talked to her,
she never talked back.
Only a few years into my drinking I began to hear voices—one was Anna's.
Her voice spoke directly behind my eyes. It was a quiet voice,
it was as if I was simply overhearing her.

I never thought it unnatural that I heard her voice, or Roethke's voice,
the other voice I heard. There is a photograph of the American poet Roethke
on the cover of his *Collected Poems*. His hair is white against a blue background.
I was almost more enthralled by the photograph
than by his poems, and I would hear his voice. This voice
felt more like the possessed, and soon
I felt more like the possessed for hearing it.
A few years later I tore the jacket/photo because of this feeling of
being possessed.

When I tore Roethke I must have torn Anna's voice—
sober or intoxicated, I heard neither voice again.
A decade later I traded my copy of *The Cantos*
for the jacket/photo of Roethke. I traded with a drinking friend.
We laughed: *The Cantos* had been a gift to me from the mother of a man
who used me.

Even on that day I did not tell my friend or anyone of the voices,
and even having Roethke's white face again did not bring back
his voice or Anna's voice. And no amount of drinking or drinking less
brought them back either.

Perhaps by tearing his face apart I had broken their spell.
It did not break the spell of drinking, but then I did not want to break
the drinking spell.

Even recurring dreams can break if you tell someone the dream.
I finally wrote a recurring dream once and that killed it.
But like the voices I then missed the dream.

Sometimes someone tells me of a recluse writer or painter,
and she or he is still drinking somewhere, or he or she is known to be
out there in a specific place but so reclusive that it doesn't matter,
whereabouts "unknown." And being an alcoholic, even in recovery, I have
this more than momentary sense that dark life isn't so bad after all.
There is an alcoholic shine to that darkness. It's enough of a longing
to make me tremble. And then I turn back, as I do here.

✗ GOODBYE,

Goodbye, no-brainer who married.
Goodbye, rider of horse of sexual no's,
Goodbye, man whose face leaned between thighs and licked and wept
    but did not mean either enough.
Goodbye, writer of antiletters and qualms.
Goodbye, misnomer of he who could find a gem in a desert and now
    writes smart verse instead
Goodbye, woman who cooks coffee until the aroma could wake the dead.
    "Coffin coffee."
Goodbye, to myself. You bring out the ghost in me.
Goodbye, to yourself, and all letters whose first rung is "l"
    instead of the tricky "h."
Man who slices poems, goodbye.
Man who murders children, animals, women, or orders them about,
    more than goodbye.
More than goodbye to anyone who kills the earth.

Moonlight to any kiss which is not
both hello and goodbye.
No, no goodbye to any kisses.
Or arms.
Or seas.
Or hearts which have been witnessing
shattered hearts too long.

Goodbye to your face, only so I can
say hello to your face.

✗ FOR MARY HACKETT

This is what I wrote before Mary died. I think I read it to her one day. I don't think she said much about it. She was saying less by then, at least to me, and often was trying to get me to eat more (I wasn't hungry) or to drink more coffee. Which meant we walked o so slowly to her kitchen more than once or twice a visit.

Mary talked much about the moon and her paintings. We both did. She told me about a man on a plane who told her how to always tell the old crescent from the new one. The old one will form a C she said, and he told her to recall it by "C you later." The moon was like a tonic for Mary, and for me. We even joked and laughed about the moon.

Mary's been dead since September, 1989. She as much as told me (more than once) to say hello to her by saying hello to the moon. So I do. Some evenings when the moon is coming along, especially a new one, I say hello, hello Mary, and some evenings when it's the old moon I wave and say, C you later.

✖ ENTIRE DILEMMA

I wish you had knocked on my door today,
because I've realized I've had the entire dilemma
upside down. It will not seem important to you,
but you see, it has not been my parents who have
made me lonely, deeply deeply cold, over many

years and bridges, it was never them at all.
All this time I thought so, but I've had the entire dilemma
upside down. It will not seem important to you,
which is why you did not knock, but it has been the town
I was born in, town my parents remained in, town I returned

to like a dead bird still flying in search of a dead bell,
a soundless one the town likes to ring coldly out into the sky
at five o'clock or six o'clock or whenever one of the important
persons wants someone less important to know they are counting
money so they ring the bell—it is the town which has made

me sick all these, a town! And it made my parents sick,
and it made my brothers sick, and it made my sisters sick,
perhaps my sisters sickest of all—for they were always the ones
who were told you have nothing to be sick about, stick around
and see. They saw! Their poor eyes hardened like coins on a shelf,

and my relatives walked into our house to count these coins,
and slowly but surely they took my sisters apart, my little sisters!
And my brothers and I have returned and returned—because my

father was there, because my mother was there, and she is still
and is now very sick indeed and old, and yet never knew

we had the entire dilemma upside down. It will not seem important
to you, but you see it has been the town all these years.
It was not the roads we loved, it was not the houses,
—we actually hated the houses but we could not tell,
we hated the roads there but we walked upon them like ghosts

of deep habit, searching for passports, illegal passports, which
would place us in another country where someone is important
for you, knocks at your door, and whispers get out, get out,
long before you have heard the rivers in the words, the words
which come close, only to stray, only to judge you like the person

you are not, like the person on the top of a bell, being told
now, now, come down, come down from your bell you little dead bird.
It is five or six o'clock. The blackbird is sewing a song for you
to wear. A heavy song. All the heavier, for it is a song you will
always wear, and wear it upside down.

It has been the town I was born in.
It has made me sick. It has killed people, over and over.
Everyone tells everyone you are nothing in my town, and it is meant.
I wish you had knocked on my door today,
because I've realized I've had the entire dilemma upside down.

BUT BEAUTIFUL

But beautiful is the dog lost,
once headed east, then later

in the dark south. But
beautiful is the cold

which never seems to stay.
Dead Robert is but beautiful,

although other than that
I know not what to say.

Never knew him. Only
in stories told to me

by Charlie does the sun
shine on Robert. And Martha

is but beautiful, though
always was the sense we

conversed in small circles,
nevertheless conversed.

And another Charlie and
another Martha, two old

cousins gone now who-
knows-where. But they

were fine, had a big
old honestly red barn

and a dog whose name
I forget who one Sunday

was attacked by a por-
cupine. But beautiful

is Jane, and Jay and
Clay. Jane is ill,

too ill to be known
for the time being.

But beautiful, like
a simple star shining

when the day is still
dying, and night

wonders if it can
get up, and out.

But beautiful is
the beginning, the

day dear, near or far.
Simple people.

Some who die, some
who die while in

your life. Some who
do violent things.

Some who are forgiven
by themselves. But

beautiful is the drive
up the river's side.

All these people
have taken it.

Like a fairy tale
in which the hero

or heroine, son
or daughter, receives

a song of grace,
a secret grace, to

bestow upon the
journey when the time

arrives. But
beautiful to retrieve

them, one by one,
and one for all.

Nancy Mitchell

The Author

Entire Dilemma is Michael Burkard's seventh collection of poetry and his first book since W.W. Norton published *My Secret Boat (A Notebook of Prose and Poems)* in 1990. He has received a Whiting Writers' Award, the Poetry Society of America's Alice Fay di Castagnola Award, and two grants from both the New York State Foundation for the Arts and the National Endowment for the Arts. He has taught at various colleges and universities, most recently the University of Louisville, LeMoyne College, and Syracuse University. During the 1990s he has also worked as an alcoholism counselor, particularly with children whose lives have been impacted by alcoholism.